YORK NOTES

CW00503874

KS2 ENGLISH SATS

3-STEP TEST BOOSTER: READING

ANNA COWPER

YORK PRESS
322 Old Brompton Road, London SW5 9JH

PEARSON EDUCATION LIMITED
Edinburgh Gate, Harlow,
Essex CM20 2JE, United Kingdom
Associated companies, branches and representatives throughout the world

First published 2018

10 9 8 7 6 5 4 3 2 1

ISBN 978–1–2922–3285–0

Typeset by Ken Vail Graphic Design Ltd
Printed in Slovakia

Text credits: Excerpt from 'Macavity: The Mystery Cat' from *Old Possum's Book of Practical Cats* by T. S. Eliot. Copyright 1939 by T.S. Eliot. Copyright (c) renewed 1967 by Esme Valerie Eliot. Reprinted by permission of Faber and Faber Ltd and Houghton Mifflin Harcourt Publishing Company. All rights reserved.

Image credits: Anonymous/Open Clip Art for page 5 and elsewhere / Rostislav Stach/ Shutterstock for page 6 bottom / Urbanbuzz/Alamy for page 9 top / 0mela/Shutterstock for page 12 / evgenii mitroshin/Shutterstock for page 15 middle / GlobalP/© iStock for page 18 top / GlobalP/© iStock for page 18 bottom / Barandash Karandashich/Shutterstock for page 21 bottom / monstergraingames/ Open Clip Art for page 24 and elsewhere / Merlin2525/ Open Clip Art for page 24 and elsewhere / illustrissima/Shutterstock for page 25 bottom / Inked Pixels/ Shutterstock for page 26 bottom / SCPhotos/Alamy for page 30 bottom / SashaA Skvortcova/ Shutterstock for page 35 bottom / Redshinestudio/Shutterstock for page 36 bottom / Ken Gillespie/Alamy for page 40 bottom / IanDagnall Computing/Alamy for page 41 middle / Brovko Serhii/Shutterstock for page 45 / 123dartist/Shutterstock for page 51 top / focal point/ Shutterstock for page 52 top / Master1305/Shutterstock for page 58 bottom / clearviewstock/ Shutterstock for page 63 / Katrina Leigh/Shutterstock for page 64 / Vuk Kostic/Shutterstock for page 69 bottom / Veronika Surovtseva/Shutterstock for page 70 bottom

CONTENTS

Section C: 20-minute tests

Answers

Record your progress!   **96**

HOW TO USE YOUR *3-STEP TEST BOOSTER: READING* BOOK

Getting up to speed for the Key Stage 2 Reading tests is as easy as 1 – 2 – 3 with this fantastic *3-Step Test Booster: Reading* book!

Test yourself in three easy steps:

STEP ONE – 10-minute tests

Quick tests to get you off to a good start!

STEP TWO – 15-minute tests

Longer tests to build your skills and stamina!

STEP THREE – 20-minute tests

Full-length practice to ensure you're ready for your Key Stage 2 test!

TOP TEST TIPS

- Time yourself or work at your own speed.
- Use the Answers at the back to get your scores.
- Record your scores with the handy Scorecards and Progress chart.
- See your skills and confidence grow!

Good luck and enjoy!

Friend fox

"Foxes are vermin," sneered cousin Jeremy. With his mean, pointy face and reddish hair, Maria thought he looked a bit like a fox himself.

"When foxes break into the chicken house, they kill everything. They're vicious and my dad has no choice but to shoot them."

Jeremy was right about the chickens. The morning after the fox raid, Maria's uncle's chicken house had been a terrible sight – full of bloody corpses and feathers. The fox had only got away with two. Maria cried, but Jeremy and Uncle Jed were furious and vowed to get revenge. They would hunt that fox down, they said, and the dogs would tear him to pieces.

"Not him," thought Maria. "Her."

All that afternoon, Maria paced up and down, restlessly, trying not to hear the barking of the hounds. Finally she went for a walk, but it was worse outside. Maria could hear the dogs crashing about in the undergrowth and they seemed to be getting nearer. And then, suddenly, there she was. Moving so fast, she was barely there, the fox shot across the path, an orange streak on the grey afternoon air.

The hounds were so close now Maria could see them, but, what was this? They were streaming away to the right of the path, towards the meadows and out of the woods. Maria smiled. Somehow, the clever she-fox had tricked them. Her den, where she lived with her four chubby red cubs, was in the opposite direction and Maria knew she was safe.

1 Look at the third paragraph.
What had a fox done that made cousin Jeremy and Uncle Jed so angry?

_____

                                                                    1 mark

2 Look at the third paragraph. **Find** and **copy two** phrases that tell us
what the inside of the chicken house looked like in the morning.

1. _____

2. _____

                                                                    1 mark

3 Maria knows the fox that killed the chickens.
Give **one** piece of evidence from the text that shows this.

_____

                                                                    1 mark

4 Look at the final two paragraphs. How does Maria's mood change?
Give evidence from the text to show her **two** different moods.

_____

_____

_____

_____

                                                                    2 marks

5 Look at the final paragraph: *Maria smiled. Somehow, the clever she-fox had tricked them.*
How does Maria feel about the fox getting away? Explain why this is.

_____

_____

_____

_____

2 marks

6 Number the events below 1–5 to show the order in which they happen in the text. The first one has been done for you.

Uncle Jed hunts the fox with the dogs. ☐

Maria sees the fox running away. ☐

The fox escapes to safety. ☐

The fox kills the chickens. 1

Uncle Jed is angry. ☐

1 mark

Well done for completing this test! Add up your marks and work out your total score.

TOTAL SCORE: .... (out of 8)

Ghost boy

Sam had left his trainers at school so he went back to fetch them. It was weird being back in the building again after everyone else had gone home. It was so quiet. Except, what was that noise? Sam opened the classroom door and was surprised to see a boy hunched over his desk crying.

"What's the matter?" Sam asked.

The boy scowled at him and rubbed his eyes furiously. He was pale with a strange, very short, slicked-back hairstyle.

"It's none of your business," he said angrily.

He had a precise, posh voice and was wearing shorts – a bit cold for December, Sam thought. He looked at the boy's book, open on the desk and saw the mark 0/10 at the top of the page with lots of teacher's writing in angry red ink.

"I'm bad at maths, too," Sam said sympathetically. He looked a bit more closely at the boy's book. "But I know how to do these kinds of sums. My mum showed me. I can help you, if you like."

"Really?" said the boy, eagerly. "I would be so grateful if you would."

Sam thought this was a rather strange, old-fashioned way of speaking, but the boy was smiling shyly at him, and he felt himself starting to like him.

"I'll go and get my maths book," he said.

He raced down the corridor to fetch it, but when he got back he found only the evening sunlight streaming through the windows across an empty desk. The boy had gone!

1 Look at the first paragraph. Why was the school quiet and empty?

Tick **one**.

It was the beginning of the day and lessons hadn't started yet. ⬭

It was the weekend and the school was shut. ⬭

It was the end of the day and lessons had finished. ⬭

1 mark

2 What happened that made Sam go into the classroom?

_____

_____

1 mark

3 *The boy scowled at him and rubbed his eyes furiously.*
What does *scowled* mean in this sentence?

_____

1 mark

4 Find **two** things that Sam thinks are strange about the boy.

1. _____

2. _____

1 mark

SECTION A: TEST 2

5 What evidence is there in the text that the boy is upset about his schoolwork? Give **three** examples.

1. _____

_____

2. _____

_____

3. _____

_____

3 marks

6 Number the following events 1–6 to show the order in which they happened. The first one has been done for you.

The boy speaks angrily to Sam. ☐

Sam hears the sound of someone crying in the classroom. ☐

Sam comes to fetch his trainers. 1

Sam offers to help the boy. ☐

The boy disappears. ☐

1 mark

Well done for completing this test! Add up your marks and work out your total score.

TOTAL SCORE: .... (out of 8)

Overheard on a saltmarsh

Nymph, nymph, what are your beads?

    Green glass, goblin. Why do you stare at them?

Give them me.

    No.

Give them me. Give them me.

    No.

Then I will howl all night in the reeds,

Lie in the mud and howl for them.

    Goblin, why do you love them so?

They are better than stars or water,

Better than voices of winds that sing,

Better than any man's fair daughter,

Your green glass beads on a silver ring.

    Hush, I stole them out of the moon.

Give me your beads, I want them.

    No.

I will howl in the deep lagoon

For your green glass beads, I love them so.

Give them me. Give them.

    No.

Harold Monro (1879–1932)

1 What **two** creatures are having a conversation in this poem?

1. _____

2. _____

_____
1 mark

2 Look at the first two lines of the poem. What does the goblin do that shows that he wants the beads?

Tick **one**

He tries to steal them. ☐

He looks at the beads for a long time. ☐

He cries. ☐

_____
1 mark

3 **Find** and **copy one** word in the poem that means to cry and moan loudly.

_____

_____
1 mark

4 Using information from the poem, tick **one** box to show whether each statement is **true** or **false**.

	True	False
The beads are made of green glass.		
The goblin loves the stars and the water more than the beads.		
The owner of the beads says they come from the moon.		
The goblin says he will steal the beads.		

_____
1 mark

5 Look at the goblin's final words, *Give them me. Give them.*
Why does he repeat the phrase *Give them*?

_____

_____

_____

1 mark

6 Do you think that the goblin will get the beads in the end?
Use evidence from the text to explain your answer.

_____

_____

_____

_____

_____

_____

3 marks

Well done for completing this test! Add up your marks and work out your total score.

TOTAL SCORE: .... (out of 8)

SECTION A: TEST 3

Living at the top of the world

The North Pole is the point that is farthest north on the planet Earth. If you look at a globe, the North Pole is right at the top and the South Pole is right at the bottom.

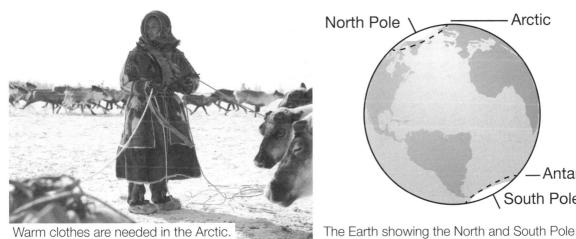

Warm clothes are needed in the Arctic.

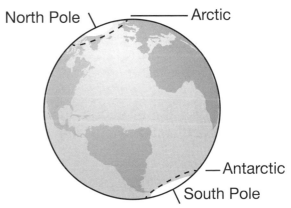

The Earth showing the North and South Pole

The region around the North Pole is called the Arctic and the region around the South Pole is the Antarctic. The Antarctic is a frozen desert because there is no water, only rocks and ice.

The Arctic, however, is a frozen ocean, surrounded by land. Animals such as seals, reindeer and polar bears live here, as well as some plants and even humans. The Inuit people in Greenland and Canada and the Sami people in Norway and Finland have found ways to adapt to the harsh climate. Their ancestors learned how to build warm houses, make warm clothes and live by hunting and fishing.

But the top of the world is a difficult place for humans to survive. It is bitterly cold in winter with temperatures so low that it hurts to breathe. The winter is not only cold but also dark. The sun does not shine for about half a year. During the short summer season, however, the sun never sets, but shines for twenty four hours a day.

For the Inuit and the Sami people, the return of the sun after winter is the most important time of the year. The entire community gathers to wait for the exact moment when the sun appears above the horizon and there are week-long celebrations.

1 Look at the first paragraph.
Which is the point that is farthest north on Earth?

_____

1 mark

2 Look at the second paragraph. Why is the Antarctic described as a desert?

_____

1 mark

3 Look at the second and third paragraphs. Tick **one** box to show whether each statement is **true** or **false**.

	True	False
The Arctic is the region around the South Pole.		
You can find polar bears, seals and reindeer living in the Antarctic.		
Inuit people live in Greenland and Canada.		
Humans traditionally survived by hunting and fishing in the region around the North Pole.		

1 mark

4 Look at the fourth paragraph, beginning: _But the top of the world ..._
Find **two** phrases which help to give the reader an idea of how extremely cold it is in at the North Pole.

1. _____

2. _____

1 mark

SECTION A: TEST 4

5 Number the following information 1–5 to show the order in which it is given in the text. The first one has been done for you.

It's very dark in the Arctic as well as very cold. ☐

The return of the sun is the most important time of the year for people in the Arctic. ☐

The Antarctic is a frozen desert. ☐

The North Pole is at the top of the Earth. 1

People have learned to survive and live in the Arctic. ☐

1 mark

6 Look at the final paragraph. Do you think the Inuit and Sami people enjoy the return of the sun after winter? Explain fully, giving evidence from the text to support your answer.

_____

_____

_____

_____

3 marks

Well done for completing this test! Add up your marks and work out your total score.

TOTAL SCORE: .... (out of 8)

The snakes of Sheptal

If you are scared of snakes, then make sure you never stay the night in Sheptal, a village in the state of Maharashtra in India.

All the houses in the village have a special resting place up in the rafters for cobras. These dangerous snakes move around people's homes as freely as cats and dogs. It's not an unusual sight to see a cobra slithering across somebody's kitchen to take a drink from a bowl of milk which has been specially left out for it. And if there is a child playing on the floor nearby, nobody is worried!

A king cobra

So how did this come about? The cobra is greatly feared by many people because it is one of the most venomous snakes in the world. A cobra bite will kill most humans within a few hours. Since there are many snakes in this hot, dry region on the plains, there are thousands of deaths from snake bites every year. But instead of hating and fearing snakes, the people of Sheptal, where no-one has been bitten, have chosen to treat them with respect.

This seems to be the secret behind the peaceful cohabitation of people and snakes, but it is unlikely that many outsiders would be able to sleep well knowing that there was a cobra in the roof!

Snakes in Hinduism – TOP FACTS!

- Snakes, especially cobras, are sacred animals in the Hindu religion.
- Snakes are a symbol of wisdom and purity.
- In some places, people believe it is their duty to welcome cobras into their homes.

1 Look at the first paragraph. In which country is the village of Sheptal?

_____

1 mark

2 *All the houses in the village have a special resting place up in the rafters for cobras.* Circle **one** correct option to complete the following sentence.

Cobras come inside people's houses to rest …

under the bed   under the roof   in the kitchen

1 mark

3 Look at the first paragraph.
In what other way do the villagers in Sheptal look after snakes?

_____

_____

1 mark

4 *And if there is a child playing on the floor nearby, nobody is worried!*
What does this tell you about the people of Sheptal?

_____

1 mark

5 Look at the section called *Snakes in Hinduism – TOP FACTS!*
Why are the people of Sheptal happy to let snakes into their houses?
Give evidence from the text to support your answer.

_____

_____

_____

_____

3 marks

6 Which of the following would be the best summary of the whole text?

Tick **one**.

Why you don't need to be scared of snakes ☐

Sheptal is a place where people have a special
relationship with snakes. ☐

Sheptal is a village where only cobras live. ☐

How to tame snakes ☐

1 mark

Well done for completing this test! Add up your marks and work out your total score.

TOTAL SCORE: .... (out of 8)

How Thor lost his hammer and got it back again

When the Norse god, Thor, had his hammer stolen from him by the cunning giant Thrym, he was in despair. The gods needed the magic hammer to protect Asgard, the realm in which they lived. Thrym said that he would return the hammer only if he could have Freya, goddess of beauty, as his wife. Thor asked his clever friend Loki to help him.

"Thrym can be cunning, but he is not very clever," said Loki. "We must pretend to take Freya to him as his bride, but I will take you instead, wearing Freya's veil and dress. Tell Thrym that the marriage can take place only when you have the hammer in your hands."

So Loki arrived in Jötunheim, where Thrym lived, bringing with him a heavily-veiled 'Freya'. Fortunately Thrym was not too surprised at his bride's height and width. He tried to lift Freya's veil, but Loki told him to wait. He said Freya might be so terrified by his hideous features that she would faint and the wedding would be delayed.

When the wedding feast began, Thor forgot himself. He enjoyed eating eight salmon straight away, followed by a whole ox. Then he drank heartily. Thrym's mother started to look at her son's bride suspiciously. Loki quickly said that it was time for the marriage ceremony, but first Thrym must put into his bride's hands the great hammer of the gods.

As soon as Thor's hand closed on the hammer, he stood up, and with one blow knocked the giant's house down. Then he strode back to Asgard with Loki by his side.

1

Look at the first paragraph.
How does Thor lose his hammer at the beginning of the story?

_____

1 mark

2

To get his hammer back again, Thor has to:

Tick **one**.

give his wife, Freya, to Thrym ⬜

let Thrym marry Freya, a beautiful goddess ⬜

ask Loki to fetch the hammer from Jötunheim ⬜

send Loki as bride for Thrym to marry ⬜

1 mark

3

Look at the third paragraph. _So Loki arrived in Jötunheim, where Thrym lived, bringing with him a heavily-veiled 'Freya'._
Why is 'Freya' heavily-veiled?

_____

_____

1 mark

4

Look at the third paragraph. **Find** and **copy one** word that means 'very ugly'.

_____

1 mark

SECTION A: TEST 6

5 *When the wedding feast began, Thor forgot himself ...*
Look at the fourth paragraph. Explain how Thor's behaviour at the feast makes Thrym's mother suspicious of him. Use evidence from the text.

_____

_____

_____

_____

3 marks

6 Below are the main events from this text. Number them 1–5 to show the order in which they appear in the text. The first one has been done for you.

Thor nearly gives himself away at the wedding feast. ⬭

Thor goes to Jötunheim disguised as a bride. ⬭

Thrym steals the hammer and Thor asks Loki for help. ⬭ 1

Thor gets his hammer back and returns to Asgard. ⬭

Loki thinks of a plan. ⬭

1 mark

Well done for completing this test! Add up your marks and work out your total score.

TOTAL SCORE: .... (out of 8)

SECTION A: SCORECARD

Congratulations! You have completed the 10-minute tests!

How did you do? Enter your score for each test in the grid below:

TEST	SCORE (out of 8)
Test 1	
Test 2	
Test 3	
Test 4	
Test 5	
Test 6	
TOTAL	**(out of 48)**

Now check out the advice below and count your lucky stars!

0–16 marks	Well done for giving it a try! Try covering over your marks and giving the 10-minute tests another go. Practice makes perfect!	
17–32 marks	Great progress! Go back to the questions you found tricky and make sure you understand the answers. Then move on to the 15-minute tests!	
33–48 marks	Fantastic – amazing work! You have conquered this section and you can move straight on to the 15-minute tests!	

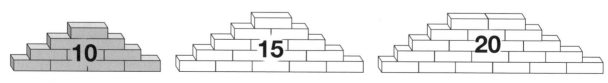

Emma's trainers

Emma has never liked me. I'm not sure why. My mum says it's because she's jealous, but she's the one with all the advantages. Who's the one with the long, shiny hair? Who has just been made captain of the netball team? Who is the prettiest, coolest, most popular girl in the class? I'll give you a clue. It's not me, plain Polly Palmer.

There's nothing at all special about me except that I can make the class laugh sometimes. I made the class laugh at Emma recently. It wasn't on purpose. I'd drawn this funny picture of Emma showing off. Art, by the way, is the *only* thing I'm any good at, and this picture somehow got passed round the class. And the best – or the worst, it depends how you look at it – was that even Mr Parker laughed when he saw it. He put on a stern face immediately afterwards, but he still laughed.

Since then, Emma has really hated me. It's kind of understandable I suppose, but that doesn't make it easier. Because if Emma isn't speaking to me, then nobody else is either. I'm officially the most unpopular person in Class Six these days.

But that still isn't enough revenge for Emma. I know this because I've just opened my locker and found some trainers inside it. I'm so shocked that I can't breathe. Ever since this morning, Emma has been complaining that her brand new trainers have gone missing. We've got PE this afternoon and it's clear what she wants to happen.

I take a deep, shuddering breath. What am I going to do? Suddenly something Mr Parker said jumps into my mind: "It's very important to be yourself."

OK, I may be unpopular and bad at sport (so why would I steal trainers?), but I am an honest person. And I stand up for myself.

I take one long, deep breath. Then I take those trainers out of my locker and set off to find Emma in the playground.

1 Look at the first paragraph. Polly lists the advantages she thinks Emma has. What is the **first** one?

_____

1 mark

2 Look at the second paragraph. What reasons might Emma have to be jealous of Polly? Give **two** reasons.

1. _____

2. _____

2 marks

3 Look at the second paragraph. Who do you think Mr Parker is?

_____

1 mark

4 **Find** and **copy one** word in the second paragraph that means 'serious and disapproving'.

_____

1 mark

5

Because if Emma isn't speaking to me, then nobody else is either.
Explain why none of the class will speak to Emma either.

_____

_____

_____

1 mark

6 When Polly finds some trainers in her locker she is:

Tick **one**.

excited and curious   ☐

angry   ☐

surprised and happy   ☐

shocked and scared   ☐

1 mark

7 What do you think Emma wants to happen in the PE lesson this afternoon? Explain your answer with evidence from the text.

_____

_____

_____

_____

2 marks

8 Number the following events 1–5 to show the order in which they happened. The first one has been done for you.

Most people in the class stop speaking to Polly. [ ]

Polly finds Emma's trainers in her locker. [ ]

Emma is made captain of the netball team. [1]

The class laughs at Polly's funny picture. [ ]

Polly draws a funny picture of Emma. [ ]

1 mark

9 *Then I take those trainers out of my locker and set off to find to Emma in the playground.*
Predict what will happen next in the story. Use evidence from the text to support your predictions.

a. What do you think Polly will do? Why?

_____

_____

b. How do you think Emma will react? Why?

_____

_____

2 marks

Well done for completing this test! Add up your marks and work out your total score.

TOTAL SCORE: .... (out of 12)

SECTION B: TEST 1

15

Climbing the highest mountain in the world

KEY FACTS

Name: *Mount Everest* (English)
           Chomolungma (Tibetan)
           Sargarmartha (Nepalese)

Location: In the Himalayas on the border between Tibet and Nepal
Height: 8848 metres

Did you know?

A) Climbing Mount Everest is extremely dangerous. The weather conditions are so bad that there are only a few weeks in the year when it's possible to climb safely. Most expeditions to the top, or summit, are in May or the first two weeks of November. Even then, terrible snowstorms can happen suddenly with freezing winds of up to 100 kilometres per hour – deadly conditions few humans can survive in!

B) Everest is a particularly difficult mountain for climbers. The rock faces are very steep and there are lots of glaciers to cross on the way up, where there's a high risk of falling into the ice. But it's the final kilometres near the summit which are the most challenging. This area is called the 'death zone' because you are so high up the atmosphere is very thin. The air only has one-third of the amount of oxygen humans need to survive.

Using a ladder to cross an open crack on Mount Everest

C) Climbers carry extra oxygen to help them breathe. But this won't prevent them becoming ill with a disease called altitude sickness, which can kill them in a few hours. Not having enough oxygen also makes climbers very tired and they find it difficult to think clearly. Twenty-five percent of the deaths on Everest happen when people are coming down from the summit because it's the time when they usually feel coldest and most exhausted.

George Mallory

So why can't we just admire this beautiful and terrible mountain? Why do so many people want to climb it? George Mallory, a British climber who died on Everest in 1924, was asked this question. His answer has become famous: "Because it's there".

Humans, it seems, cannot just look at a mountain, particularly if they know it's the highest one in the world; they have to find out if they can get to the top.

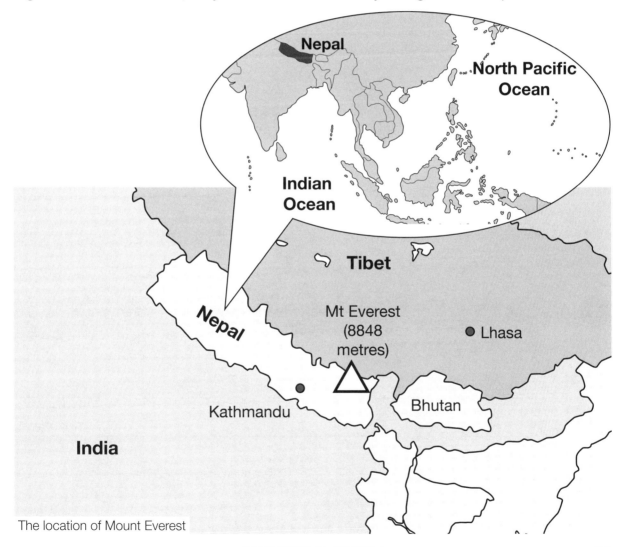

The location of Mount Everest

1 Read the *KEY FACTS* box.
Which **two** countries is Mount Everest on the border between?

1. _____

2. _____

‾‾‾‾‾
1 mark

2 **Find** and **copy one** word in paragraph A) that means the top of a mountain.

_____

‾‾‾‾‾
1 mark

3 Look again at paragraph A). Would it be a good idea to go an expedition to climb Mount Everest during the month of August? Explain your answer.

_____

_____

‾‾‾‾‾
2 marks

4 Look at paragraph B). Find **three** reasons why Mount Everest is an especially difficult mountain to climb.

1. _____

2. _____

3. _____

‾‾‾‾‾
2 marks

SECTION B: TEST 2

5 Look at paragraph C). Tick **one** box in each row to show whether each statement is **true** or **false**.

Climbers on Everest …

	True	False
… can take extra oxygen with them to help them breathe.		
… are not at risk from altitude sickness if they have enough oxygen.		
… are more likely to have an accident on the way up than on the way down.		

1 mark

6 *So why can't we just admire this beautiful and terrible mountain?*
Find and **copy one** positive and **one** negative word used to describe Mount Everest in this sentence.

Positive word:

_____

Negative word:

_____

2 marks

7 What do you think motivated George Mallory to climb Mount Everest? Explain your answer with reference to the text.

_____

_____

_____

_____

2 marks

8 Below are some summaries of different sections from this text. Number them 1–5 to show the order in which they appear in the text. The first one has been done for you.

The dangers of not having enough oxygen ⬜

Why Everest is so difficult to climb ⬜

The location, height and different names of Mount Everest 1

Why so many people want to climb Everest ⬜

When expeditions to climb Mount Everest are possible ⬜

1 mark

Well done for completing this test! Add up your marks and work out your total score.

TOTAL SCORE: .... (out of 12)

SECTION B: TEST 2

TEST 3

The story of Ekalavya the archer

This story happened 5,000 years ago in India when a boy named Ekalavya longed to study archery with the great teacher, Drona. He went to Drona's Gurukul, or training school, but Drona refused to teach him. Prince Arjuna, who was Drona's pupil, told Ekalavya condescendingly that the noble art of archery was not for Shudra, the caste of labourers to which Ekalavya belonged, but was reserved for princes and nobles.

So Ekalavya went home and used mud from the river to make a statue of Drona. Day after day he took his bow and arrow, worshipped the statue and practised shooting. In time, his perseverance and faith transformed Ekalavya into a great archer.

One day, a barking dog disturbed Ekalavya's practice so he shot seven arrows in rapid succession into the dog's mouth. The arrows wedged the dog's mouth open so it couldn't bark. Drona got to hear about this and wanted to meet the archer capable of such a feat. Ekalavya was found and brought before Drona who was astonished to hear that Ekalavya considered him to be his teacher: his statue had taught Ekalavya to shoot.

When Prince Arjuna heard this he became angry.

"You promised that you'd make me the best archer in the world!" he accused Drona. "But now a common *Shudra* has become better than me!"

Drona didn't want to break his promise to the prince, so he demanded that Ekalavya cut off his right thumb as his *dakshina*, the payment that the pupil gives his teacher at the end of his training. For a moment Ekalavya stood silent. Without his thumb he could never shoot arrows again. But the teacher must be satisfied. Without further hesitation, Ekalavya drew out his knife and cut off his thumb!

Drona was humbled and blessed the young archer for his courage.

"Ekalavya, even without your thumb, you are a great archer. I bless you for your loyalty to your teacher."

Despite his disability, Ekalavya continued to practise archery. He learned to shoot arrows with his index and middle finger and became an even greater archer than before.

SECTION B: TEST 3

1 Look at the first paragraph.
Ekalavya longed to study archery with the great teacher, Drona.
Why do you think Drona did not want to accept Ekalavya as his pupil?

_____

_____

1 mark

2 Look at the second paragraph. Tick the best definition of archery.

shooting with a bow and arrow ☐

using a weapon to shoot things ☐

shooting with a spear ☐

1 mark

3 Look at the second paragraph.
What **two** things did Ekalavya do every day after he went home?

1. _____

2. _____

2 marks

4 Look at the third paragraph.
Find and **copy one** short phrase that means 'quickly one after the other'.

_____

1 mark

5 Look at the third paragraph.
Why was the dog who had been disturbing Ekalavya unable to bark?

_____

_____

1 mark

6 Using information from the text, tick **one** box in each row to show whether each statement is **true** or **false**.

	True	False
Drona was surprised to discover that he was Ekalavya's teacher.		
Prince Arjuna was jealous of Ekalavya.		
Drona didn't want to break his promise that he would make the prince the best archer in the world.		

1 mark

7 Look at the paragraph beginning: _Drona didn't want to break …_
What does Drona ask Ekalavya for as payment for his teaching?

_____

_____

1 mark

SECTION B: TEST 3

8 How do you think Drona felt about Ekalavya before and after Ekalavya cut off his own thumb? Explain your answer with reference to the text.

_____

_____

_____

_____

_____

3 marks

9 Which is the best summary of Ekalavya's character?

Tick **one**.

He is talented but lazy. ☐

He likes reading more than being active. ☐

He is hard-working and brave. ☐

He does not respect the prince. ☐

1 mark

Well done for completing this test! Add up your marks and work out your total score.

TOTAL SCORE: .... (out of 12)

The king in the car park

A skeleton found by archaeologists excavating a car park in Leicester has been proved to be the body of an English king. King Richard III was killed over 500 years ago during the Battle of Bosworth Field. His death marked the end of a thirty-year-long civil war, in which two families, the Yorks and the Lancasters, fought for the English throne. As Richard of York was the loser, it was assumed that his body was lost on the battlefield.

The experts who examined the skeleton established that it had a badly curved spine and was of a man between twenty and thirty years old. These findings excited historians as Richard III died when he was thirty-two years old and was known to have had a hunched back. The owner of the skeleton had suffered ten injuries around the time of death, including two potentially fatal skull wounds that could have been made by a heavy weapon such as a sword or battle axe.

Scientists traced a living descendant of Richard III living in London. His DNA – a substance in every cell of the body which carries information about a person's identity – matched the DNA from the bones in the car park. Historians believe that this is conclusive proof of the skeleton's identity as the dead king.

Archaeologists at work

After Richard was killed in the battle in 1485, it seems that his body was buried hastily in the centre of Leicester in what was then Greyfriar's Church, the site of the present-day car park. His skeleton was reburied in Leicester Cathedral in 2015. This time, he was given a proper king's funeral, attended by members of the royal family and a whole cathedral full of mourners.

Who was Richard III?

Richard III - a royal portrait

- Richard lost his father, uncle and a brother in battle when he was just eight years old.
- He became king after the death of his elder brother, Edward, in 1483.
- Richard had one of the shortest reigns in English history: 26 months.
- He was the last English king to die in battle. He was killed by the army of the future Henry VII.

1 Look at the first paragraph. How did King Richard III die?

_____

1 mark

2 *A skeleton found by archaeologists excavating a car park in Leicester ...*
Explain the meaning of the word *excavating* in this sentence.

_____

_____

1 mark

3 Look at the first paragraph.
Who would Richard III have been fighting against? How do you know?

_____

_____

_____

2 marks

4 Look at the second paragraph. What **two** things about the skeleton made historians connect it to Richard III?

1. _____

2. _____

1 mark

5 Put a tick in the correct box to show whether each of the following statements is a **fact** or an **opinion**.

	Fact	Opinion
Richard fought bravely and well in the battle.		
He died as a result of terrible injuries.		
Richard III had one of the shortest reigns in English history.		
He didn't deserve to lose the battle.		

2 marks

6 What do we know from the second paragraph about how Richard died? Give evidence from the text for your answer.

_____

_____

_____

2 marks

7 *Scientists traced a living descendant of Richard III living in London.*
Tick the best meaning of *descendant* below.

Someone who is an expert on royal families ◯

A friend who lived a long time ago ◯

Someone who is related to someone who lived a long time ago ◯

1 mark

SECTION B: TEST 4   43

8 Look at the information in the box *Who was Richard III?*
What is special about the way that Richard III died?

_____

_____

1 mark

9 Below are some summaries of different paragraphs from this text.
Number them 1–5 to show the order in which they appear in the text.
The first one has been done for you.

The skeleton's two burials 500 years apart ☐

Where the skeleton was found and who it belonged to 1

More information about King Richard III's life
from his childhood to his death ☐

How historians proved who the skeleton was ☐

What the owner of the skeleton looked like and how he died ☐

1 mark

Well done for completing this test! Add up your marks and work out your total score.

TOTAL SCORE: .... (out of 12)

Extract from
Macavity: The Mystery Cat

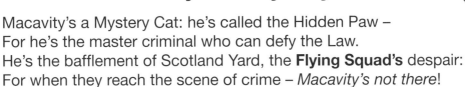

Macavity's a Mystery Cat: he's called the Hidden Paw –
For he's the master criminal who can defy the Law.
He's the bafflement of Scotland Yard, the **Flying Squad's** despair:
For when they reach the scene of crime – *Macavity's not there*!

Macavity, Macavity, there's no one like Macavity,
He's broken every human law, he breaks the law of gravity.
His powers of levitation would make a **fakir** stare,
And when you reach the scene of crime – *Macavity's not there*!
You may seek him in the basement, you may look up in the air –
But I tell you once and once again, *Macavity's not there*!

Macavity's a ginger cat, he's very tall and thin;
You would know him if you saw him, for his eyes are sunken in.
His brow is deeply lined with thought, his head is highly domed;
His coat is dusty from neglect, his whiskers are uncombed.
He sways his head from side to side, with movements like a snake;
And when you think he's half asleep, he's always wide awake.

Macavity, Macavity, there's no one like Macavity,
For he's a fiend in feline shape, a monster of depravity.
You may meet him in a by-street, you may see him in the square –
But when a crime's discovered, then *Macavity's not there*!

He's outwardly respectable. (They say he cheats at cards.)
And his footprints are not found in any file of Scotland Yard's
And when the larder's looted, or the jewel-case is rifled,
Or when the milk is missing, or another **Peke's** been stifled,
Or the greenhouse glass is broken, and the trellis past repair –
Ay, there's the wonder of the thing! *Macavity's not there*!

Macavity, Macavity, there's no one like Macavity,
There never was a Cat of such deceitfulness and suavity.
He always has an alibi, and one or two to spare:
At whatever time the deed took place – MACAVITY WASN'T
THERE!

T. S. Eliot (1888–1965)

Glossary

fakir –   a type of Holy man from India or the Far East who can also perform
incredible acts such as seeming to make themselves invisible or float in
the air.

Flying Squad – a police division that goes quickly to the scene of a serious crime.

Peke – a Pekinese, a small breed of dog with long hair, popular as a pet.

---

1 *For he's the master criminal who can defy the law*. Who is Macavity? Tick the **one** correct answer.

A cat who commits crimes ⃝

A cat who is a detective and solves mysteries ⃝

A cat who has disappeared ⃝

1 mark

2 *He's the bafflement of Scotland Yard, the Flying Squad's despair:*
Explain the meaning of *bafflement* in this sentence.

_____

1 mark

3 Give two places that are mentioned in the second verse where you *won't* find Macavity.

1. _____

2. _____

2 marks

4 How do you know from the second verse that Macavity is very good at jumping high off the ground? Explain with evidence from the text.

_____

_____

_____

2 marks

5 Look at the third verse. Tick **one** box in each row to show whether each statement is **true** or **false**.

	True	False
Macavity is a short, thin animal.		
He frowns a lot in a thoughtful way.		
He has a high, round forehead and sunken eyes.		
His fur is shiny and well brushed.		

1 mark

6 *He sways his head from side to side, with movements like a snake;*
Find **another** clue in the third verse that suggests Macavity could be dangerous and you shouldn't trust him.

_____

_____

1 mark

7 Draw lines to match the descriptions of different crimes with the examples from the fifth verse. The first one has been done for you.

stealing precious objects   *the larder's looted*

destroying the garden fence   *the jewel case is rifled*

stealing food   *another Peke's been stifled*

killing other animals   *the trellis past repair*

1 mark

8

Macavity, Macavity, there's no one like <u>Macavity</u>,
He's broken every human law, he breaks the law of <u>gravity</u>.
Look at the second verse, fourth verse and the final verse. **Find** and **copy**
three words that rhyme with Macavity and that have the following meanings.
The first one has been done for you.

1. a force that makes things fall to the ground _____gravity_____

2. great politeness and pleasantness _____

3. total wickedness _____

2 marks

9

Number the information below 1–3 to show the order in which it is given
in the poem.

Macavity's sinister appearance ☐

Introduction to Macavity the master criminal cat ☐

A list of Macavity's crimes ☐

1 mark

Well done for completing this test! Add up your marks and work out your total score.

TOTAL SCORE: .... (out of 12)

SECTION B: SCORECARD

Congratulations! You have completed the 15-minute tests!

How did you do? Enter your score for each test in the grid below:

TEST	SCORE (out of 12)
Test 1	
Test 2	
Test 3	
Test 4	
Test 5	
TOTAL	**(out of 60)**

Now check out the advice below and count your lucky stars!

0–20 marks	Well done for giving it a try! Try covering over your marks and giving the 15-minute tests another go. Practice makes perfect!	
21–40 marks	Great progress! Go back to the questions you found tricky and make sure you understand the answers. Then move on to the 20-minute tests!	
41–60 marks	Fantastic – amazing work! You have conquered this section and you can move straight on to the 20-minute tests!	

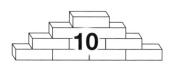  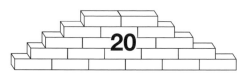

Cut and polished diamonds

Diamonds

Diamonds and how they are made

Diamonds are rare and valuable precious stones. One of the reasons they are so highly valued is that incredibly powerful forces are needed to create them. Every diamond starts out as piece of carbon, which will have been deep under the Earth's crust for millions of years, where it is very hot and there is a lot of heavy weight pushing down on it. As a result of the intense heat and pressure the atoms of a diamond are very tightly bonded together – this gives diamonds their hard and shiny quality.

Sources of diamonds

The first diamonds were found in India. It is thought they were being mined in India as long ago as 400 BCE! For thousands of years, diamonds have been used not just to make jewellery but also in tools and machines. They can cut through both metal and stone. For a long time, diamonds were very expensive because they were only found in India. But at the beginning of the 19th century, lots of diamonds were discovered in South Africa, and so the price started to go down. Until that time, only kings and queens and extremely rich people had diamond jewellery, but as diamonds gradually became cheaper, more people could afford them.

Diamonds for ordinary people

De Beers, a big South African diamond-mining company, decided it needed to do something about the falling prices of diamonds. In 1948 it started an advertising campaign with the slogan 'A diamond is forever' which helped to make diamond rings more popular as engagement rings.

A diamond ring

In the USA, the sales of diamond rings and jewellery went up by nearly 50% and diamond engagement rings are still popular today.

Artificial diamonds: frequently asked questions

Q: What is the difference between real and artificial diamonds?

A: Artificial diamonds have exactly the same structure as real diamonds and the same qualities. The only difference is that they are made in a laboratory. It is impossible to tell the difference between an artificial diamond and a real one without special equipment.

Q: Are artificial diamonds better than real ones?

A: The first artificial diamonds were yellow in colour and people didn't find them as attractive as real diamonds. The production process improved, however, and it is now possible to make artificial stones which are completely clear and as attractive as real diamonds. They are also 30–40% cheaper.

Q: Will artificial diamonds replace real diamonds in the future?

A: In the future, more diamonds will be created in laboratories because new ways of using diamonds are being discovered. In medicine, for example, they are used in eye operations and to help treat serious diseases. But real diamonds will probably continue to be used for jewellery, even though they are not as perfect as artificial diamonds. Even the best and finest examples of real diamonds have a small flaw somewhere. However, this is considered by many people to be what makes a real diamond special. The flaw is always different, so no two diamonds are ever the same.

1 *Diamonds are rare and valuable precious stones.*
Which word below is closest in meaning to rare?

Tick **one**.

strange ☐

uncommon ☐

expensive ☐

beautiful ☐

1 mark

2 Look at the first paragraph. Which **two** qualities of diamonds are the result of them being under intense heat and pressure beneath the Earth's crust?

1. _____

2. _____

2 marks

3 Look at the section *Sources of diamonds*. Why do you think diamonds are used in tools and machine parts? Give evidence from the text to support your answer.

_____

_____

_____

_____

2 marks

4 Look at the section *Sources of diamonds*.
When and why did diamonds start becoming less expensive?

_____

_____

1 mark

5 Look at the section *Diamonds for ordinary people*.
Why do you think the diamond company De Beers wanted to advertise
its diamonds?

_____

_____

1 mark

6 What is the connection in the text between diamonds and getting married?
Give evidence from the text to support your answer.

_____

_____

_____

2 marks

7 Look at the section *Artificial diamonds: Frequently asked questions.*
What was the problem with the first artificial diamonds?

_____

_____

‾‾‾‾‾‾
1 mark

8 Put a tick in the correct box to show whether each of the following
statements is a **fact** or an **opinion**.

	Fact	Opinion
Artificial diamonds are not as attractive as real diamonds.		
Real diamonds are more expensive than artificial ones.		
You need special equipment to distinguish an artificial diamond from a real one.		
Real diamonds are the best for jewellery.		

‾‾‾‾‾‾
1 mark

9 *Even the best and finest examples of real diamonds have a small flaw
somewhere.* What is the meaning of *flaw* in this sentence?

_____

_____

‾‾‾‾‾‾
1 mark

10 How does the flaw in real diamonds help to make them special?
Give evidence from the text to support your answer.

_____

_____

_____

‾‾‾‾‾‾
2 marks

11 Draw lines to match each section to its main content.
One has been done for you.

Section	Content

Section

- Diamonds and how they are made
- Sources of diamonds
- Diamonds for ordinary people
- Artificial diamonds: frequently asked questions

Content

- Talks about how more people started buying diamonds and they became popular.
- Contrasts the similarities and differences between artificial and real diamonds.
- Gives information about where diamonds have been found and different things they are used for.
- Gives information about how diamonds are formed.

1 mark

12 Which phrase best describes what the whole text is about?

Tick **one**.

Diamonds and how to make them ☐

How real and artificial diamonds are made and what they are used for ☐

The history of artificial diamonds and how they have replaced real ones ☐

Why artificial diamonds will never be as good as real ones ☐

1 mark

Well done for completing this test! Add up your marks and work out your total score.

TOTAL SCORE: .... (out of 16)

SECTION C: TEST 1

TEST 2

Attitude

Winston Jones is not the youngest, but certainly the smallest and lightest (some would say scrawniest) junior boxer in the club. He zips down the stairs into the club's back entrance. He doesn't want Coach to notice him arriving late again, doesn't need another lecture about his bad attitude. He shoots along the long row of lockers and explodes into the changing room like a rocket on bonfire night.

The changing room is empty. That's bad since it means that training has started. But it's good because there are no other kids around to notice that Winston isn't doing any changing. The thing is, the clothes he's wearing are the only ones he has. He takes off his hoodie and puts his dreadlocks into an elastic band. His T-shirt is OK, but, there's a problem: he can't box wearing his jeans.

He remembers the crate of clothes in Coach's office.
"This stuff's here for people to borrow," Coach had said, carefully not looking in Winston's direction, "if they forget their kit".

A few seconds later, Dan, 'The Man', Johnson, boxing champion, local bad-boy-made-good, back in his old club to see the new talent, watches this skinny Rasta boy strutting into the junior training area. The boy's red shorts, much too big for him, are bunched round his waist and flare out like a ballet skirt. He's ten minutes late.

"Jones, you're late again!" yells Coach.

"Yes, Boss," bawls back Winston, nose in the air, looking totally unrepentant.

"That's the kid you told me about, right?" says Dan The Man, not looking impressed.

"Yes, indeed," says Coach, sighing.

Dan The Man watches out of the corner of his eye as Winston warms up: skipping at the speed of light and attacking the pads like an unfed tiger. For the sparring, Coach pairs Winston with a big, muscular kid, almost twice his weight. But the kid never gets near him. Winston dances round him, light as a mosquito, supple as a snake, only zooming in for the sting. The big kid limps away at the end of the match, nursing his bruised face and Winston watches him go, a sneer twisting his face.

SECTION C: TEST 2   57

By this time, Dan The Man can't take his eyes off him.

"The kid's good, but he's got a bad attitude," he says to Coach. "Call him over."

"Jones! Come here. Dry yourself off first."

Coach throws Winston a towel. He throws it slightly high and, as Winston leaps with his usual grace to catch it, his much-too-big ballet dancer's skirt of a pair of shorts succumbs to gravity and falls to his ankles.

The club explodes with laughter and jeers. Just for a moment, Winston looks very small and young. Looks like he's going cry. But then, he flings his red shorts over his arm like a bullfighter's cape and strides across the hall, proud as a young prince. "You want to talk to me, Boss?"
"I want to talk to you," says Dan The Man. "You can box and you've got a good attitude – to some things."

1

Look at the first paragraph.
Where do the events of the story *Attitude* take place?

Tick **one**.

in a school ☐

in a boxing club ☐

in a circus ring ☐

in a sports centre ☐

1 mark

2

Look at the first paragraph. **Find** and **copy two** words which show that Winston is in a hurry.

1. _____

2. _____

1 mark

3

What do we know about Winston's appearance after reading the first two paragraphs? Find two things.

1. _____

2. _____

1 mark

SECTION C: TEST 2   59

4 Look at the second paragraph.
Why is Winston relieved to find the changing room empty?

_____

_____

1 mark

5 Look at the second paragraph.
What can you guess about Winston's home life?
Explain your answer making reference to the text.

_____

_____

_____

_____

2 marks

6 *"This stuff's here for people to borrow," Coach had said, carefully not looking in Winston's direction, "if they forget their kit".*
Why do you think coach is careful not to look at Winston when he is talking about the clothes?

_____

_____

_____

1 mark

7 Look at the paragraph beginning: *A few seconds later ...*
Why has Dan The Man come to this particular place to look for new boxing talent?

_____

_____

___
1 mark

8 *"Yes, Boss," bawls back Winston, nose in the air, looking totally unrepentant.*
What does *unrepentant* mean in this sentence? Tick **one** box.

confident ☐   ashamed ☐   not sorry ☐

___
1 mark

9 *"That's the kid you told me about, right?" says Dan The Man.*
"Yes, indeed," says Coach, sighing.
Why do you think Coach sighs at this point in the story?

_____

_____

___
1 mark

10 *... skipping at the speed of light and attacking the pads like an unfed tiger ...*
What **two** impressions does this description give you of how Winston does his training?

1. _____

2. _____

___
2 marks

11 Number the following events 1–5 to show the order in which they happen. The first one has been done for you.

Coach throws Winston a towel and he loses his shorts trying to catch it. ☐

Winston is happy to find that he is alone in the changing room. ☐

Dan the Man speaks to Winston. ☐

Winston arrives very late and in a hurry. 1

Dan the Man sees Winston winning a fight. ☐

1 mark

12 How and why does Dan The Man change his opinion of Winston during the story? Explain your answer with evidence from the text.

_____

_____

_____

_____

_____

3 marks

Well done for completing this test! Add up your marks and work out your total score.

TOTAL SCORE: .... (out of 16)

SECTION C: TEST 2

TEST 3

A Smuggler's Song

If you wake at midnight, and hear a horse's feet,
Don't go drawing back the blind, or looking in the street,
Them that ask no questions isn't told a lie.
Watch the wall my darling while the Gentlemen go by.

Five and twenty ponies,
Trotting through the dark –
Brandy for the Parson, **'Baccy** for the Clerk.
Laces for a lady; letters for a spy,
Watch the wall my darling while the Gentlemen go by!

Running round the **woodlump** if you chance to find
Little barrels, roped and tarred, all full of brandy-wine,
Don't you shout to come and look, nor use 'em for your play.
Put the **brishwood** back again – and they'll be gone next day!

If you see the stable-door setting open wide;
If you see a tired horse lying down inside;
If your mother mends a coat cut about and tore;
If the lining's wet and warm – don't you ask no more!

If you meet King George's men, dressed in blue and red,
You be careful what you say, and mindful what is said.
If they call you "pretty **maid**," and chuck you 'neath the chin,
Don't you tell where no one is, nor yet where no one's been!

Knocks and footsteps round the house – whistles after dark –
You've no call for running out till the house-dogs bark.
Trusty's here, and *Pincher's* here, and see how dumb they lie
They don't fret to follow when the Gentlemen go by!

If you do as you've been told, 'likely there's a chance,
You'll be give a dainty doll, all the way from France,
With a cap of **Valenciennes**, and a velvet hood –
A present from the Gentlemen, along 'o being good!

Five and twenty ponies,
Trotting through the dark –
Brandy for the Parson, 'Baccy for the Clerk.
Them that asks no questions isn't told a lie –
Watch the wall my darling while the Gentlemen go by!

Rudyard Kipling (1865–1936)

Glossary

'Baccy – tobacco
brishwood – piece of firewood
maid – a young girl
Valenciennes – a kind of lace made in France
woodlump – pile of firewood

SECTION C: TEST 3

1 In the first verse of the poem, what should you *not* do if you are woken up at night by the sound of a horse's feet?

_____

1 mark

2 *Watch the wall my darling while the Gentlemen go by.*
What does the instruction *watch the wall* mean in this sentence?
Tick **one** box.

While the smugglers ride past, you should:

stay behind the wall ⬚

not watch them ⬚

hide behind the wall and watch carefully ⬚

turn your back to the wall ⬚

1 mark

3 *Five and twenty ponies,*
Trotting through the dark –
Why do you think the smugglers are riding in the dark?

_____

1 mark

4 Look at the second verse.
Find **four** things that the *Five and twenty ponies* are carrying.

1. _____   2. _____

3. _____   4. _____

1 mark

SECTION C: TEST 3

5

Running round the woodlump if you chance to find
Little barrels, roped and tarred, all full of brandy-wine,

Explain **two** things the poem says you shouldn't do if you find barrels of brandy.

1. _____

2. _____

6

Draw lines to match the quotations to what they might give away about the smugglers' activities.

If you see a tired horse lying down

If the lining's wet and warm

If your mother mends a coat cut about and tore

Someone was bleeding from a wound.

Someone's clothes were damaged in a fight.

Someone had to ride fast to escape.

7

If you meet King George's men, dressed in blue and red.

Who do you think King George's men are?

Tick **one**.

soldiers ☐

princes ☐

prisoners ☐

8 Look at the fifth verse. Why does it say that you should be careful when you talk to King George's men?
Explain your answer with evidence from the poem.

_____

_____

_____

2 marks

9 *Trusty's here, and Pincher's here, and see how dumb they lie*
They don't fret to follow when the Gentlemen go by!

a. Who are *Trusty* and *Pincher*?

_____

b. Explain the meaning of *don't fret to follow*.

_____

2 marks

10 Who is the poem addressed to and how do you know?
Explain your answer with evidence from the poem.

_____

_____

_____

3 marks

11

If you do as you've been told, 'likely there's a chance,
You'll be give a dainty doll, all the way from France,
Tick the word or phrase below that is closest in meaning to *dainty*.

Tick **one**.

fussy ☐

small and pretty ☐

fragile ☐

expensive ☐

1 mark

12 What is the main message of the poem?

Tick **one**.

Smugglers are dangerous and will attack you. ☐

Watch and help the smugglers. ☐

Ignore the smugglers and pretend you haven't
seen them. ☐

Don't repeat what the smugglers say. ☐

1 mark

Well done for completing this test! Add up your marks and work out your total score.

TOTAL SCORE: .... (out of 16)

The runaways

The trolls arrived in the village just as it was getting light. They liked to take people by surprise when they were still hazy with sleep, their reactions slow. Some of the villagers never got the chance to wake up properly that day. Probably the only reason why I'm still here is because my brother, Samuel, used to rising early to work in the fields, saw them coming. He was up on the roof of the abandoned house where we had slept that night, tracing our best route to the border. He saw a big group of trolls running silently in formation through the woods and watched in horror as they descended on the village like a pack of wolves.

But the worst moment was when a small group of three broke off from one of the columns of running trolls and began to jog towards the abandoned house. As Samuel saw this, he said later, his whole body turned to ice. He ran to shake me awake.

"Alex! There are trolls coming this way! We've got to hide!"

Where could we hide? We looked around desperately. In the years of war and famine, people had stripped the inside of the house of anything and everything they could burn or exchange for food, leaving it an empty box. The single remaining object was a big, heavy desk. I don't know why it hadn't been carried off for firewood; maybe because it was made of extremely heavy, tropical wood. It also seemed to be fixed to the floor … but marvellously, unbelievably, it was hollow inside.

We crammed ourselves into that tiny space. We pushed Peter, being the smallest, in first. We didn't have to tell him he needed to be quiet. As soon as he heard the word 'trolls' his eyes became as huge as saucers and his bottom lip began to wobble. Samuel lay on the floor across the middle of the space and I packed myself in on top of him. My neck was twisted uncomfortably and my face was turned upwards and partly exposed, but it was too late to move. We could already hear the trolls' heavy footsteps.

The footsteps came nearer and harsh voices rang out in the still, morning air. They were walking round the building. They were leaving. No, they were coming back! The ground vibrated as heavy boots walked right up to the front of the desk; the wood creaked as a heavy body leant over it and then, suddenly, a bloodshot eye in a pale, upside-down face was staring at me, only a few centimetres from my face. I saw the eye widening with surprise and the long, dark lashes that surrounded it flaring apart. Time stopped. I think that I fainted or lost consciousness from sheer terror because everything went black.

When the blackness cleared, the upside-down face had gone. A harsh voice said something in a dismissive tone and we felt the feet walking away again, receding into the distance, until all was quiet again and still.

SECTION C: TEST 4

1 Look at the first paragraph. What time of day is it when the story begins?

Tick **one**.

midnight ☐

very early in the morning ☐

towards the middle of the day ☐

late evening ☐

1 mark

2 *They liked to take people by surprise when they were still hazy with sleep.*
Explain the meaning of *hazy with sleep* in this sentence.

_____

_____

1 mark

3 *Some of the villagers never got the chance to wake up properly that day.*
What do you think happened to these people?

_____

_____

1 mark

4

Look at the first paragraph.
What were the children doing in the abandoned house?

_____

_____

1 mark

5

They descended on the village like a pack of wolves.
What does this description suggest about the trolls? Give **two** suggestions.

1. _____

2. _____

2 marks

6

Look at the second paragraph: ... *his whole body turned to ice* ...
What does this show about how Samuel feels?

_____

1 mark

7

Look at the fourth paragraph beginning: *Where could we hide? We looked around desperately ....*
Why is there nothing left inside the abandoned house?

_____

_____

_____

1 mark

SECTION C: TEST 4

8 Look at the fifth paragraph beginning: *We crammed ourselves into ...*
What evidence is there in the text to suggest that Peter is quite young?
Explain your answer fully with reference to the text.

_____

_____

_____

_____

2 marks

9 Look at the fifth paragraph. **Find** and **copy two** expressions which mean
'fitting things with difficulty into a small space'.

1. _____

2. _____

1 mark

10 Draw lines to match each element of the story with the correct quotation
from the text. The first one has been done for you.

Where the story takes place	*Alex! There are trolls coming this way!*
Warning of danger	*We crammed ourselves into that tiny space.*
Reaction to the danger	*the abandoned house where we had slept that night*
Most dramatic moment	*a bloodshot eye in a pale, upside-down face was staring at me*

2 marks

SECTION C: TEST 4

11 The title of the story is *The runaways*.

a. What do you think the children are running away from?

_____

_____

b. Where are they running to? Support your answer with evidence from the text.

_____

_____

3 marks

12 Below are some summaries of different paragraphs from this text. Number them 1–5 to show the order in which they appear in the text. The first one has been done for you.

The trolls leave the abandoned house. ⬜

A troll sees Alex in his hiding place. ⬜

The children manage to find a hiding place. ⬜

The children look for somewhere to hide in the abandoned house. ⬜

Samuel sees the trolls arriving. [1]

3 marks

Well done for completing this test! Add up your marks and work out your total score.

TOTAL SCORE: .... (out of 16)

SECTION C: SCORECARD

Congratulations! You have completed the 20-minute tests!

How did you do? Enter your score for each test in the grid below:

TEST	SCORE (out of 16)
Test 1	
Test 2	
Test 3	
Test 4	
TOTAL	**(out of 64)**

Now check out the advice below and count your lucky stars!

0–21 marks	Well done for giving it a try! Try covering over your marks and giving the 20-minute tests another go. Practice makes perfect!	
22–43 marks	Great progress! Go back to the questions you found tricky and make sure you understand the answers.	
44–64 marks	Fantastic – amazing work! You have conquered this section.	

Test 1 – Friend fox

1. 1 mark

A fox had got into the chicken house and killed lots of chickens.

2. 1 mark for both correct:

- *a terrible sight*
- *full of bloody corpses and feathers*

3. 1 mark

Maria shows she knows the fox because she knows the fox is female, not male: *"Not him," thought Maria. "Her."*

4. Up to 2 marks

In paragraph 3 Maria is restless and worried: *Maria paced up and down, restlessly, trying not to hear the barking of the hounds.* (**1 mark**)

In paragraph 4 Maria is happy: *Maria smiled.* (**1 mark**)

5. Up to 2 marks

Maria feels happy about the fox getting away: *Maria smiled. Somehow, the clever she-fox had tricked them.* (**1 mark**)

She is happy because she knows the fox is a mother with four cubs: *Her den, where she lived with her four chubby red cubs, was in the opposite direction and Maria knew she was safe.* (**1 mark**)

6. 1 mark for the correct order:

1 The fox kills the chickens.

2 Uncle Jed is angry.

3 Uncle Jed hunts the fox with the dogs.

4 Maria sees the fox running away.

5 The fox escapes to safety.

Test 2 – Ghost boy

1. 1 mark

It was the end of the day and lessons had finished.

2. 1 mark

He went into the classroom because he heard a noise: *Except, what was that noise?*

3. 1 mark

Scowled means that he scrunched up his forehead/frowned deeply/put on an angry expression.

4. 1 mark for two correct points.

Any two of:

- His strange, very short, slicked-back hairstyle.
- He was wearing shorts – a bit cold for December.
- He had a rather strange, old-fashioned way of speaking.

5. Up to 3 marks. 1 mark each for any of the following points.

We can tell that the boy is upset about his schoolwork because:

- He was crying.
- He got a mark out of 0/10 for his maths.
- He is happy to accept Sam's offer to explain how to do the sums.
- He is angry: "It's none of your business," he said angrily.

6. 1 mark for the correct order:

1 Sam comes to fetch his trainers.

2 Sam hears the sound of someone crying in the classroom.

3 The boy speaks angrily to Sam.

4 Sam offers to help the boy.

5 The boy disappears.

Test 3 – Overheard on a saltmarsh

1. 1 mark

A nymph and a goblin.

2. 1 mark

He looks at the beads for a long time.

3. 1 mark

howl

4. 1 mark for all four correct:

	True	False
The beads are made of green glass.	✓	
The goblin loves the stars and the water more than the beads.		✓
The owner of the beads says they come from the moon.	✓	
The goblin says he will steal the beads.		✓

5. 1 mark

The goblin repeats the phrase *Give them* to try to persuade/put pressure on the nymph.

6. Up to **3 marks** (1 mark for the point; 2 marks for the point plus one piece of evidence; 3 marks for the point plus two pieces of evidence).

Point: It is likely that the goblin will never get the beads. (**1 mark**)

Evidence:

• The nymph keeps on saying no. (**1 mark**)

• All the goblin can do to persuade the nymph is to say that he will cry if he doesn't get them – he has no way of forcing the nymph to do what he wants. For example:
I will howl in the deep lagoon
For your green glass beads, I love them so. (**1 mark**)

Test 4 – Living at the top of the world

1. 1 mark

The North Pole.

2. 1 mark

The Antarctic is described as a desert because there is no water there:
There is no water, only rocks and ice.

3. 1 mark for all four correct:

	True	False
The Arctic is the region around the South Pole.		✓
You can find polar bears, seals and reindeer living in the Antarctic.		✓
Inuit people live in Greenland and Canada.	✓	
Humans traditionally survived by hunting and fishing in the region around the North Pole.	✓	

4. 1 mark for two correct phrases:

- *It is bitterly cold in winter*
- *it hurts to breathe*

5. 1 mark for the correct order:

1 The North Pole is at the top of the Earth.

2 The Antarctic is a frozen desert.

3 People have learned to survive and live in the Arctic.

4 It's very dark in the Arctic as well as very cold.

5 The return of the sun is the most important time of the year for people in the Arctic.

6. Up to **3 marks**

The Inuit and Sami people enjoy the return of the sun because:

- It comes after months of winter darkness when it is dark all day and all night. (**1 mark**)
- The whole community gathers together to wait for the sun to rise. (**1 mark**)
- There are week-long celebrations. (**1 mark**)

SECTION A: ANSWERS

Test 5 – The snakes of Sheptal

1. 1 mark

India

2. 1 mark

under the roof

3. 1 mark

They give them milk to drink. *It's not an unusual sight to see a cobra slithering across somebody's kitchen to take a drink from a bowl of milk which has been specially left out for it.*

4. 1 mark

It shows that the people of Sheptal are not afraid of snakes but have learned to live with them.

5. Up to **3 marks** (1 mark for the point; 2 marks for the point plus one piece of evidence; 3 marks for the point plus two pieces of evidence).

Point: The people are happy to have the snakes in their houses because, as Hindus, they believe snakes are sacred animals. (**1 mark**)

Evidence:

- *Snakes are a symbol of wisdom and purity.* (**1 mark**)
- *In some places, people believe it is their duty to welcome cobras into their homes.* (**1 mark**)

6. 1 mark

Sheptal is a place where people have a special relationship with snakes.

Test 6 – How Thor lost his hammer and got it back again

1. 1 mark

His hammer was stolen by a giant called Thrym.

2. 1 mark

let Thrym marry Freya, a beautiful goddess.

3. 1 mark

'Freya' is heavily-veiled to disguise the fact that it is really Thor.

4. 1 mark

hideous

5. Up to **3 marks** (1 mark for the point; 2 marks for the point plus one piece of evidence; 3 marks for the point plus two pieces of evidence).

Point: Thor behaves in a way that is not ladylike. (**1 mark**)

Evidence:

- He eats eight salmon straight away and a whole ox. *He enjoyed eating eight salmon straight away, followed by a whole ox.* (**1 mark**)

- He drinks heartily. *Then he drank heartily.* (**1 mark**)

6. 1 mark for the correct order:

1 Thrym steals the hammer and Thor asks Loki for help.

2 Loki thinks of a plan.

3 Thor goes to Jötunheim disguised as a bride.

4 Thor nearly gives himself away at the wedding feast.

5 Thor gets his hammer back and returns to Asgard.

Test 1 – Emma's trainers

1. 1 mark

She has long, shiny hair: *Who's the one with the long, shiny hair?*

2. Up to 2 marks

- She is funny: *There's nothing at all special about me except that I can make the class laugh sometimes.* (**1 mark**)

- She is good at drawing: *Art, by the way, is the only thing I'm any good at.* (**1 mark**)

3. 1 mark

Mr Parker is probably the class teacher or art teacher.

4. 1 mark

stern

5. 1 mark

Emma is the most popular girl in the class so if she isn't speaking to Polly, other people will be afraid to.

6. 1 mark

shocked and scared

7. Up to 2 marks

Point: Emma wants people to see her trainers in Polly's locker and to believe that Polly has stolen them. (**1 mark**)

Evidence: Emma wants revenge because everyone laughed at Polly's drawing of her. *But that still isn't enough revenge for Emma. I know this because I've just opened my locker and found some trainers inside it.* (**1 mark**).

8. 1 mark for the correct order:

1 Emma is made captain of the netball team.

2 Polly draws a funny picture of Emma.

3 The class laughs at Polly's funny picture.

4 Most people in the class stop speaking to Polly.

5 Polly finds Emma's trainers in her locker.

9. Up to **2 marks**

a Polly has the trainers in her hand and is going to find Emma in the playground. It is likely that she is going to give the trainers back to Emma and confront her about putting them in her locker: *I am an honest person. And I stand up for myself.* (**1 mark**)

b Emma will probably try to accuse Polly of stealing the trainers and deny that she put them in the locker. She will lie because she hates Polly and wants other people not to like her. *Since then, Emma has really hated me.* (**1 mark**)

Test 2 – Climbing the highest mountain in the world

1. 1 mark for both correct:

Tibet and Nepal

2. 1 mark

summit

3. Up to **2 marks**

Point: No. This is because the weather conditions would be too dangerous in the summer months (most expeditions take place in May or November). (**1 mark**)

Evidence: *The weather conditions are so bad that there are only a few weeks in the year when it's possible to climb safely. Most expeditions to the top, or summit, are in May or the first two weeks of November.* (**1 mark**)

4. 1 mark for any two points below, **2 marks** for all three points:

- *The rock faces are very steep*

- There are lots of glaciers to cross where you can fall into the ice: *there are lots of glaciers to cross on the way up, where there's a high risk of falling into the ice.*

- It's difficult to breathe near the top as there isn't enough oxygen: *The air only has one-third of the amount of oxygen humans need to survive.*

5. 1 mark for all three correct:

Climbers on Everest …

	True	False
… can take extra oxygen with them to help them breathe.	✓	
… are not at risk from altitude sickness if they have enough oxygen.		✓
… are more likely to have an accident on the way up than the way down		✓

6. Up to **2 marks**

Positive word: *beautiful* (**1 mark**)

Negative word: *terrible* (**1 mark**)

So why can't we just admire this beautiful and terrible mountain?

7. Up to **2 marks**

Point: He wanted the challenge of knowing if he could get to the top of the highest mountain in the world. (**1 mark**)

Evidence: George Mallory said it was *"Because it's there"*. *Humans, it seems, cannot just look at a mountain, particularly if they know it's the highest one in the world; they have to find out if they can get to the top.* (**1 mark**)

8. 1 mark for the correct order:

1 The location, height and different names of Mount Everest

2 When expeditions to climb Mount Everest are possible

3 Why Everest is so difficult to climb

4 The dangers of not having enough oxygen

5 Why so many people want to climb Everest

Test 3 – The story of Ekalavya the Archer

1 1 mark for either answer:

Because he was from a low caste/social class. He was only a labourer, not a prince or a noble.

2. 1 mark

shooting with a bow and arrow

3. Up to 2 marks:

- worshipped the statue of Drona: *worshipped the statue* (**1 mark**)

- practised shooting his bow and arrow: *and practised shooting* (**1 mark**)

4. 1 mark

in rapid succession

5. 1 mark

Because the arrows wedged or held its mouth open: *The arrows wedged the dog's mouth open so it couldn't bark.*

6. 1 mark for all three correct:

	True	False
Drona was surprised to discover that he was Ekalavya's teacher.	✓	
Prince Arjuna was jealous of Ekalavya.	✓	
Drona didn't want to break his promise that he would make the prince the best archer in the world.	✓	

7. 1 mark

To cut off his right thumb.

8. 3 marks for both points, supported with evidence from the text.
2 marks for both points, with one supported by evidence from the text.
1 mark for both points, with no supporting evidence from the text.

Point (before). Any of the following:

- Drona might have been impressed at how good an archer Ekalavya was and surprised that he had taught himself to shoot by looking at a statue.

- He may also have felt proud that his statue had inspired such a great archer.

- He might have looked down on Ekalavya because he was just a labourer, not a noble or a prince.

Evidence:
- *Drona didn't want to break his promise to the prince*

- *Drona who was astonished to hear that Ekalavya considered him to be his teacher: his statue had taught Ekalavya to shoot.*

- The prince says: *"But now a common Shudra has become better than me!"*

Point (after): Afterwards, he admired Ekalavya and thought he was brave.

Evidence: *Drona was humbled and blessed the young archer for his courage.*

9. 1 mark

He is hard-working and brave.

SECTION B: ANSWERS

Test 4 – The king in the car park

1. 1 mark

Richard III died in battle.

2. 1 mark

Excavating means digging up (in order to try and find objects from the past).

3. Up to **2 marks:**

Richard would have been fighting against the Lancaster family. (**1 mark**)

We know this because there was a civil war between the York and Lancaster families and Richard was Richard of York. ... *a thirty-year-long civil war, in which two families, the Yorks and the Lancasters, fought for the English throne. As Richard of York was ...* (**1 mark**)

4. 1 mark for both correct:

- It had a curved spine – and Richard III *was known to have had a hunched back.*

- The skeleton was of a man between twenty to thirty years of age – and *Richard III died when he was thirty-two years old.*

5. 2 marks for all four correct:

	Fact	Opinion
Richard fought bravely and well in the battle.		✓
He died as a result of terrible injuries.	✓	
Richard III had one of the shortest reigns in English history.	✓	
He didn't deserve to lose the battle.		✓

6. Up to **2 marks**

Point: He probably died from injuries to the head from a sword or battle axe. (**1 mark**).

Evidence: We know this because the skeleton had *two potentially fatal skull wounds that could have been made by a heavy weapon such as a sword or battle axe.* (**1 mark**).

7. 1 mark

Someone who is related to someone who lived a long time ago.

8. 1 mark

He was the last English king to die in battle.

9. 1 mark for the correct order:

1 Where the skeleton was found and who it belonged to

2 What the owner of the skeleton looked like and how he died

3 How historians proved who the skeleton was

4 The skeleton's two burials 500 years apart

5 More information about King Richard III's life from his childhood to his death

Test 5 – Macavity: The Mystery Cat

1. 1 mark

A cat who commits crimes.

2. 1 mark

Bafflement means not understanding something at all/having absolutely no idea about something/being totally unable to explain something. The police (Scotland Yard and the Flying Squad) can't understand or explain how Macavity manages to do what he does.

3. 2 marks for any two correct:

You won't find Macavity:

- at the scene of a crime
- down in the basement
- up in the air.

4. Up to 2 marks for two of the following:

- his feet are not on the ground: *he breaks the law of gravity* (1 mark)
- he seems to raise himself into the air: *His powers of levitation* (1 mark)
- People look up for him: *you may look up in the air* (1 mark)

5. 1 mark for all four correct:

	True	False
Macavity is a short, thin animal.		✓
He frowns a lot in a thoughtful way.	✓	
He has a high, round forehead and sunken eyes.	✓	
His fur is shiny and well brushed.		✓

6. 1 mark

He often pretends/looks as if he's half asleep, but he's always wide awake and watching: *And when you think he's half asleep, he's always wide awake.*

7. 1 mark for all four correct:

stealing precious objects → *the jewel case is rifled*

destroying the garden fence → *the trellis past repair*

stealing food → *the larder's looted*

killing other creatures → *another Peke's been stifled*

8. 2 marks

a suavity (1 mark)

b depravity (1 mark)

9. 1 mark for the correct order:

1 Introduction to Macavity the master criminal cat.

2 Macavity's sinister appearance.

3 The list of Macavity's crimes.

Test 1 – Diamonds

1. 1 mark

uncommon

2. Up to 2 marks:

- hard (**1 mark**)
- shiny (**1 mark**)

3. Up to 2 marks

Point: Diamonds are used in tools and machine parts because they are strong/sharp. (**1 mark**)

Evidence: *They can cut through both metal and stone.* (**1 mark**)

4. 1 mark

Diamonds started becoming less expensive at the beginning of the 19th century. This was because lots of diamonds were discovered in South Africa and the price went down.

5. 1 mark

Because prices had gone down they needed to find a way to get more people to buy diamonds.

6. Up to 2 marks

Point: After the De Beer's advertising campaign, diamonds became popular in engagement rings. (**1 mark**)

Evidence: *In 1948 it started an advertising campaign with the slogan 'A diamond is forever' which helped to make diamond rings more popular as engagement rings.* (**1 mark**)

7. 1 mark

The first artificial diamonds were yellow in colour and not as attractive as real diamonds.

8. 1 mark for all four correct:

	Fact	Opinion
Artificial diamonds are not as attractive as real diamonds.		✓
Real diamonds are more expensive than artificial ones.	✓	
You need special equipment to distinguish an artificial diamond from a real one.	✓	
Real diamonds are the best for jewellery.		✓

9. 1 mark

An imperfection or fault that stops it from being perfect.

10. Up to **2 marks**

Point: The flaw means that every real diamond is special because it is unique/different. (**1 mark**)

Evidence: *The flaw is always different so no two diamonds are ever the same.* (**1 mark**)

11. 1 mark for all correctly matched:

Diamonds and how they are made ➔ Gives information about how diamonds are formed.

Sources of diamonds ➔ Gives information about where diamonds have been found and different things they are used for.

Diamonds for ordinary people ➔ Talks about how more people started buying diamonds and they became popular.

Artificial diamonds: frequently asked questions ➔ Contrasts the similarities and differences between artificial and real diamonds.

12. 1 mark

How real and artificial diamonds are made and what they are used for.

Test 2 – Attitude

1. 1 mark

in a boxing club

2. 1 mark for two of the following:

- *zips*
- *shoots*
- *explodes*

3. 1 mark for any two correct:

- He is small: *certainly the smallest* (**1 mark**)
- He looks thin/weak: *and lightest (some would say scrawniest)* (**1 mark**)
- He wears his hair in dreadlocks: *and puts his dreadlocks into an elastic band* (**1 mark**)

4. 1 mark

He is relieved because there is nobody to see that he doesn't have any sports kit/boxing gear to change into.

5. Up to **2 marks**

Point: We can guess that he must come from a family without much money/a poor family (**1 mark**).

Evidence: This is because he's only got one set of clothes: *The thing is, the clothes he's wearing are the only ones he has.* (**1 mark**)

6. 1 mark

Coach doesn't want to let people know that Winston might need these clothes to change into or make it seem as if the clothes are especially for him.

7. 1 mark

Because he comes from this area (he is local) and this is his old club: *local bad-boy-made-good, back in his old club to see the new talent …*

8. 1 mark

not sorry

9. 1 mark

He might be worried that Jones won't impress Dan the Man because Jones is *late again.*

10. Up to **2 marks**

- *skipping at the speed of light* – this means that he moves very fast. (**1 mark**)
- *attacking the pads like an unfed tiger* – he is boxing in a very fierce/aggressive way. A tiger is wild animal and if it hasn't been fed it would be especially fierce. (**1 mark**)

11. 1 mark for the correct order:

1 Winston arrives very late and in a hurry.

2 Winston is happy to find that he is alone in the changing room.

3 Dan the Man sees Winston winning a fight.

4 Coach throws Winston a towel and he loses his shorts trying to catch it.

5 Dan the Man speaks to Winston.

12. Up to **3 marks**

At the start of the story, Dan The Man thinks Winston has a bad attitude because he arrives late and doesn't seem to be sorry: *"That's the kid you told me about, right?" says Dan The Man, not looking impressed.* (**1 mark**)

After watching Winston, Dan the Man is impressed with his boxing, but thinks he has a bad attitude as Winston sneers at the person he beats: *"The kid's good, but he's got a bad attitude,"* (**1 mark**)

At the end of the story, Dan the Man is impressed when Winston reacts bravely and recovers quickly when his shorts fall down and everyone laughs: *"You can box and you've got a good attitude – to some things."* (**1 mark**)

SECTION C: ANSWERS

Test 3 – A Smuggler's Song

1. 1 mark

You shouldn't push back the blind to look out of the window to see who it is: *Don't go drawing back the blind, or looking in the street …*

2. 1 mark

not watch them

3. 1 mark

The smugglers don't want anyone to see them, so they arrive at night.

4. 1 mark for all four correct:

- brandy: *Brandy for the Parson*
- 'baccy (tobacco): *'Baccy for the Clerk.*
- laces: *Laces for a lady*
- letters: *letters for a spy*

5. 1 mark for both correct:

- You shouldn't show them to people/ tell people to come and look at them: *Don't you shout to come and look …*
- You shouldn't play with them/use them in your games: *nor use 'em for your play…*

6. 1 mark for all three correct:

If you see a tired horse lying down ➔ Someone had to ride fast to escape.

If the lining's wet and warm ➔ Someone was bleeding from a wound.

If your mother mends a coat cut about and tore ➔ Someone's clothes were damaged in a fight.

7. 1 mark

soldiers

8. Up to 2 marks

Point: You should be careful you don't give them any information that could help the soldiers find the smugglers. (**1 mark**)

Evidence: You shouldn't tell the soldiers where the smugglers are or where they have been: *Don't you tell where no one is, nor yet where no one's been!* (**1 mark**)

9. 2 marks

a Trusty and Pincher are dogs.

b *… don't fret to follow* means that they aren't keen to go after the smugglers.

10. Up to **3 marks** (1 mark for the point; 2 marks for the point plus one piece of evidence; 3 marks for the point plus two pieces of evidence).

Point: The poem is addressed to a girl or child. (**1 mark**)

Evidence:

- We know it is addressed to a child because they are warned not to play with the barrels: *nor use 'em for your play*. Children, not adults, play.

- We know it is addressed to a child because the smugglers might give a doll as a reward for being good and a doll is a child's toy.

- We know it is addressed to a girl because the soldiers call her maid, which means young girl.

11. 1 mark

small and pretty

12. 1 mark

Ignore the smugglers and pretend you haven't seen them.

Test 4 – The runaways

1. 1 mark

very early in the morning

2. 1 mark

hazy with sleep means the people would be confused and have slow reactions because they had not yet woken up properly.

3. 1 mark

People didn't have the chance to wake up because they were killed by the trolls.

4. 1 mark

They had spent the night/slept there: *… the abandoned house where we had slept that night …*

5. 2 marks for two correct

Comparing them to wolves suggests that:

- they are ferocious/fierce

- they well-organized (working together in a pack)

- they want to kill because when wolves hunt in a pack it is to kill their prey.

6. 1 mark

It shows that Samuel is very frightened of the trolls.

7. 1 mark

Because it is a time of famine and war. People have taken everything from the abandoned house to burn or exchange for food.

In the years of war and famine, people had stripped the inside of the house of anything and everything they could burn or exchange for food, leaving it an empty box.

8. 1 mark for one correct, **2 marks** for any two correct:

- Peter is the smallest: *We pushed Peter, being the smallest, in first.*

- Samuel and Alex usually have to tell him to be quiet: *We didn't have to tell him he needed to be quiet.*

- He is so frightened of the trolls he starts crying: *his eyes became as huge as saucers and his bottom lip began to wobble.*

9. 1 mark for both correct:

- *We crammed ourselves into that tiny space.*

- *I packed myself in on top of him.*

10. 1 mark for all four correct:

Where the story takes places ➔ *the abandoned house where we had slept that night*

Warning of danger ➔ *Alex! There are trolls coming this way!*

Reaction to the danger ➔ *We crammed ourselves into that tiny space.*

Most dramatic moment ➔ *a bloodshot eye in a pale, upside-down face was staring at me*

11. Up to 3 marks

a The children are running away from famine, war and the trolls. (**1 mark**)

b They are trying to get to the border which suggests that they are trying to escape into another country. *He was up on the roof of the abandoned house where we had slept that night, tracing our best route to the border.* (**2 marks**)

12. 1 mark for the correct order:

1 Samuel sees the trolls arriving.

2 The children look for somewhere to hide in the abandoned house.

3 The children manage to find a hiding place.

4 A troll sees Alex in his hiding place.

5 The trolls leave the abandoned house.

RECORD YOUR PROGRESS!

Congratulations! You have completed all the tests!

How did you do overall? Enter your score for each test in the grid below, then add them together to reveal your Grand Total:

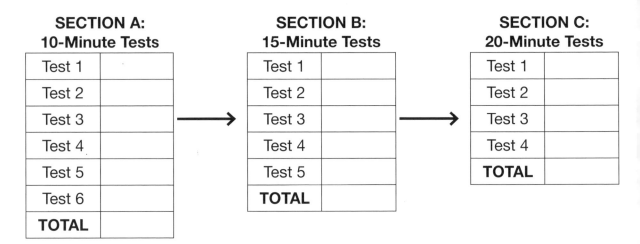

SECTION A:
10-Minute Tests

Test 1	
Test 2	
Test 3	
Test 4	
Test 5	
Test 6	
TOTAL	

SECTION B:
15-Minute Tests

Test 1	
Test 2	
Test 3	
Test 4	
Test 5	
TOTAL	

SECTION C:
20-Minute Tests

Test 1	
Test 2	
Test 3	
Test 4	
TOTAL	

GRAND TOTAL: .... (out of 172)

Now check out the advice below and count your awards!

0–50 marks	You're getting there! Find the tests that you found hardest and give them another go – with a little practice your skills will improve!	
51–120 marks	Great progress! Re-read any questions you found trickier than others – can you improve your marks this time?	
121–172 marks	Fantastic – amazing reading skills! Why not try re-taking the tests just before your SATs to make sure you're on top?	

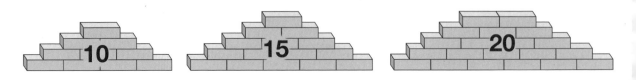